HONEY IN THE DARK

HONEY IN THE DARK

POEMS

Lee Colin Thomas

BRIGHTHORSE
BOOKS

© 2021 Lee Colin Thomas
All rights reserved.
Printed in the United States of America

Brighthorse Books
13202 N River Drive
Omaha, NE 68112
brighthorsebooks.com

ISBN: 978-1-944467-27-2

Cover Photo © Markus Spiske on Unsplash
Author Photo © J. Arthur Anderson

For permission to reproduce selections from this book, contact the editors at info@brighthorsebooks.com.

Brighthorse books are distributed to the trade through Ingram Book Group and its distribution partners. To learn more about Brighthorse Books, go to brighthorsebooks.com.

For Jean and the zookeeper

Contents

ONE
   Earthlings 3
   Here and Hiding 4
   Late Radius 5
   Indiana Corn 6
   Lodging 7
   Likelihoods, Sequels & Spinoffs 8
   As Language 9
   A Mischief Within 11
   Disembark 12
   Reservations 13
   Guest of the Lacuna 15
   In the Garden 16
   Among the Cicadas 17
   X-ray 18
   Conference Hotel Restaurant,
      Facing the Ocean 19

TWO
   Last Acre 23
   Landing at Night 24
   The Light in Florence 25
   Powers 27
   Lifeguard 28
   View of the Fairway 29
   Late Summer 31
   Arrival 32
   Amerikaner Abroad 33

Memory & the Body   34
Too Early to Tell All Secrets   35
This Might Sustain Us   36
Tourists at Duomo di Siena   37
Closer to the Mountain   38
Borrowed   39
You Must Be Told You Are a Firefighter   40
New Territory   41
Deer, as in a Dream   42

THREE
Going Somewhere   45
Given Honey in the Dark   46
Moon Stories   48
Driving in West St. Paul, Which is South
    of St. Paul but West of South St. Paul   49
The Night Watchman Ends His Shift   51
Cooking Pasta for My Parents   52
Not When the Milk   54
A Rare Find   56
Maps   57
Because They are Mine, I Wish to Visit   58
Postscript   60
November, Minneapolis   61
A Completion   62
Etymology at Dusk   63
Art Class   64

Other worlds were possible.
Other worlds were likely.

LAURA JENSEN

ONE

EARTHLINGS

We attend the weddings of happy strangers.
Friend of a friend makes for a convenient
plus one. We accept all manner of invitation
and dress the part. Standing in the midnight shine
of our best shoes, we speak with several people
we'll never see again. In the candle-lit corners
of a room collapsed past daylight,
this is what it's like, being here. Knowing
one is less important than the polished rings
someone chose to wreathe every napkin.
There's little to do but smile and wait
for the next thing to go ahead and happen.
Our obligation is small, to see the evening through.
If we pause to chat with an elegant guest by the bar,
what's the harm? There are the rare occasions
when we turn out to be something like respite
to one another. Around here, some doors stand ajar.
Past the rented speakers cueing Kool & the Gang,
one beckons. Outside, cigar and pine and gasoline
from a fleet of idle golf carts scent the air. Like us,
night has nowhere else it needs to be.

HERE AND HIDING

Of course birds, those present songs. Bells
        hung in the neighbor's yard.
Here, cut grass under foot, gasoline
        aftertaste mixed with sweat.
Squirrels gather fallen fruit
        from under the raspberry bush
while the day lilies watch a plane
        bawl away overhead.

In between these layers must exist
        finer folds and pockets
my circus senses cannot detect.
        My clumsy ears hear only
hammer on wood, but not
        into the hammer, into the wood.
My fingers are too thick
        to caress the texture of light.

My eyes too feeble to focus
        on the film of life
that must thrive inside
        light bending color
into a civilization of yellow, a destination
        all its own. One that hums
the industry of summer
        and invites me to visit

the next strange place
        I might like to live.

LATE RADIUS

After bread and salad, salt of olives
slick with gin. After evening-smeared
plates stacked in the sink,
                      I step outside
to sound the radius of a night. To test
how far afield it goes. My tongue quiets
with what passes for prayer: a few
lines rolled inside the open halls
of a breath.
                      Neighboring houses
go dark as paper bag luminarias
snuffed below the black broom-heads of trees
that rush toward, rush away, while the far-
off sparks of first kisses
thrash in snares.
                      Echoes catch
in the rooftop satellite dish: calls of cousins
I knew as children, years lived
inside a milky relay of messages
across an untraveled country.
                      I count cool
June grass among the reasons
I want to feel small: fetal walnut
in a shell, wound of happiness
open to air.

INDIANA CORN

Sometimes when I come into an unknown place
so familiar, all I want is to be able to say
its proper name. Not the one spelled out

by map or atlas, but the name that says
where I was, and also, who I was
just then, the time of day, the season

and the kind of light that evening when
the sun collapsed across stalks grown
elbow-high and better, in fields split

by county roads marked for 55.
Where millions of deep green leaves
caught the sun in their funnels

as if for a pyre. The name for that place,
the day dying, for everything I thought about
as the car continued on, carrying me

through mid-life—impossible, isn't it?
Given all there is to do, and my child
self still fresh enough in heart

to rend the ecology of memory.
For who I was, once. Drawing fence lines
around secret places, unseen in the world.

How can I leave him to stand and scare
the little hungers bound to come
for whatever's left? Without marker or alias

I might never find him again.

LODGING

There could be a latch somewhere
that comes undone and then lets out
the moths and mice and cottonwood
lives I've been thinking about
during bus rides to the office.
I remember a library book my
sister and I checked out repeatedly
one very cold winter. Pictures
of dollhouse furniture made from
spools, matchboxes, Sucrets tins
and other odds and ends
from around the house. We went
room to room in search of multi-
colored twist ties, thumbtacks
and baby food jars filled with buttons.
But nothing we constructed
had quite the same charm
as the well-appointed shoeboxes
of the frog and chipmunk figurines
we read about. We were hard
on ourselves; being children
we assumed the job of world-making
as seriously as tying a shoelace
or learning to dive at the pool.
We painted cardboard houses
fit with cellophane windows, perfect
for looking out on tissue-paper shrubs
in the yard. I still can't decide
where I really want to live: in this house
with its mortgage and too much Ikea,
or the one furnished in bottlecap
end tables, postage stamp paintings
hung on the wall, a family of finches
neighboring next door.

LIKELIHOODS, SEQUELS & SPINOFFS

There's one where I go to parties, don't study at all.
One where I walk off the job. Easy

ones where I'm rich and talented, criminally
handsome and very, very funny.

The mix-or-match game goes on: the year abroad
turns into two, then five, then eight.

I make all green lights. Never pick up a pamphlet.
I move a month earlier. The letter gets lost

in the mail. I love a woman, I am a
woman, sometimes. Living in

old apartments, my name still on the lease.
I learn to play cello. Then I learn to live

inside the music of bow against string.
I'm happy there, I think.

Later I move to a villa by the sea
and polish my little phrases

for the grocer and the baker, every day,
until the words glow like olive skins.

Sometimes I'm carried away by the wind
in a dandelion-boned body.

In one, a child finds me in the yard, and I lift
this nameless, voiceless body into my arms.

Eventually, I'm as tall as a bear in the cold,
thick on my appetite for salmon, beer and smoke.

AS LANGUAGE

Born as vibrations in a box,
as *thistle, cone,* or *plums.*

Catapulted by lift and flick
of some athletic tongue.

Travel a waved journey, take joy
in the flight. One's shape

flares again and again. One's
shape the singular thing.

Whether ridge-backed *artist arrested*
or swooping *jungle gym*

or lip-line thin *emblem,*
the murmur of *my first tattoo.*

Hold that shape until received
in the cathedral chambers

of the ear's conchal halls.
There, one shudders lastly

satisfaction at having been
received and understood,

even remembered.
No spiraling mistake

misheard, misspoke,
but shape

maintained
against the drum, going on

into echoes, another
little afterlife.

A MISCHIEF WITHIN

Unclasp the flesh from this hour, the hour
from its season, the leather strap

that cinches me inside this
body, this gravity. What could I see

once loosened? As a scarf that flies
in the wind, or a mirror that swallows

the slow colors of a violet
potted on the sill. The motion and shadow

of what we call lives: bowed heads
of horses by firelight, and nervous little dogs

in the painting on the wall. What I want
is to be one of those birds

in the margins, longing for absolution.
Not from sin, from limits, from sameness.

My ideas about wings, pipette
mechanisms of filament and frost—

Let them find strength enough
to carry my weight from the frame.

DISEMBARK

Return home, through a side door
into the kitchen
where a dish towel and absolute stillness
hang waiting, and the last-used glass
stands dry in the rack.

Arrive in time
to see an hour of daylight
pressed between the lips
of the mini blinds.
A welcome silence.

In the refrigerator find
more than expected: two beers
standing tough among the condiments.
Uncap the cool offer
that lisps from the bottle-mouth.

This re-inhabiting of a life, the climb
back inside a scaffold of furniture
and art. A few career-quality planks
nailed through
with numbers and accounts.

For now, leave all switches
untouched, heads bowed. Wait
for the dark. Feet propped
on a suitcase full of shirts
in need of washing.

Take another swig, a loose
mouthful of light in a room.

RESERVATIONS

Once a week at lunch with coworkers
from Japan and Malaysia, Hong Kong and Korea.

Once a week over beers with the guys
after volleyball at the Y.

Once a month at a potluck dinner party
for old pals and new neighbors, mismatched

platters and plates on the table. We take comfort
in the buttress of an elbow.

We are in our thirties
and pausing to eat:

the bread someone learned how to bake,
a salad of pears and soft chèvre,

desserts we don't think we should taste.
We pass on one thing after another:

the parmesan, the butter,
the promotion.

We're buying houses
and trying to get pregnant.

We're due for a raise
and need more insurance.

We are hairless
from the chemotherapy.

We're stocking the cupboards.
We have surgery scheduled.

We are without a country
and waiting

for a green card
or the next election.

We carry divorce papers and a pen
in the side pocket of a messenger bag.

We're moving again.
We're rethinking our investments.

GUEST OF THE LACUNA

All of us together in a room
and the sun coming in. So strong
it felt as if light had been born
there on the floor. I stood and read aloud,
*a family becomes fossilized—a darker crosshatch
etched in hard sand.* I wanted to believe it then,
after the funeral, and later, after the last dried
corners of the casseroles were pried loose
and reheated. I don't think anyone knew
what I was talking about. We were pencil marks
hashed across the white field of those three days,
clustered at times. Eventually
everyone went back to make some money
like the rest of the world. No one disagreed,
so I stayed in her house, sat in the few rooms
longer than planned. The scaffolding of a week's
schedules fell away. Something in me wanted to say
we have not built a life until we rebuild it,
reluctant as I was, to face the faint collection of tasks
that awaited me, in my own city, miles away.
At night the late news blossomed in spores
across screens. In every house, people stood
backlit inside window frames. The roads mostly
empty at that hour, but still, always
a chance to be seen, in passing.

IN THE GARDEN

I found a bird lying still, and I stumbled sideways, the way death
often makes us. The way it leaves a mark on even the smallest
among us: wing bent backward, head cocked too far
to be right. Pulled from the air, left in the leaves.

Every day I brought water to the impatiens struggling in the heat.
I stepped carefully and bent to peer at the body, four inches
of feathers brown as tree bark, a few shots of red
threaded through the wings.

Then the rain came and things grew without me. I watched
morning glories overtake the fence. I cut zinnias for the table.
I mowed the lawn and cleaned the garage and hosted cookouts.
I had my own summer and forgot. Until pulling weeds

on my knees, I found the skeleton tangled in the creeping Jenny.
The bones and joints like a pattern of candle drippings.
The skull, separate now. I picked it up
and held it in my palm

to inspect the watch-work jaw and nasal cavities, eye sockets, and beak.
I set it back among the leaves and imagined lying down, right there,
wingless and tired, ready for the lawn to unfold and gather me up
against the pulse and heat of earth.

AMONG THE CICADAS

If I say the brain is an organ, consciousness
a bright tangle of thread attractive to wind,
would that explain the fear? Living inside

this summer of death: My friend's father.
A forgotten classmate from long ago.
The childhood neighbor who trusted me

to feed her silvery cat when she was away.
Here in the yard, I can sense all around
that feathery moment when

the garden curls its long neck
inward, and inevitably away from,
becoming.

Every few minutes, a cicada
buzzes high in the leaves
like a spear through metal,

so deafening is their need.
How to live with such hunger?
Never can I be loved enough,

world. World, you know
what it's like: whole body ready
to rattle itself loose on a dare.

X-RAY

After the accident, pain wanted to be seen.
Only the aperture of a machine upstairs
could spot the slim notch
scored into the driftwood mantle
of my right collar bone.
The technician left me

in the room with this part of myself
aglow on the screen. No mention
of the ribs—slow swipes of icing
on a layer cake, shallow drifts
of snow on the rim of a garden pot
left out too long. Nor the pottery
scapula or the long-handled
spoons hung to each side.

They have names, I remembered: *radius, ulna*.
But I saw the cross-work of kite frames. A cello bow.
The bunched white peony bud
of the skull, and the hatched-open jaw. A body
more beautiful than the strict illustration
posted on the wall. Mine
clattered its pieces like a wind chime

as I reached for my shirt, unfurled
its cotton folds between these miniature
chandeliers. Each knuckle of light
warmed in an instant. Enough to hold
each button, a hammer, any pen,
every doorknob.

CONFERENCE HOTEL RESTAURANT, FACING THE OCEAN

Limp napkins on the next terrace table
signal the departure of humans. Alone
I am dismissed as mere shadow
in the canvas shade of the canopy
when a fraternity hazing of wings
flares in the salt mist over the railing
and lands, inches from my elbow.
The crow allows a pugilist glance
my way, before turning to survey
the wasted gobs of yolk, spit-damp
crusts, and a murderous smear of jam
on a serrated blade. Beyond sand,
another appetite as angry and quiet
as any surviving body. The crow
beaks a fat, untouched sausage link,
cigar-thick and half as long. What other reason
to pause here? Before my resting hands,
a few ceramic pools of sky
catch another edge of vastness
and push back.

TWO

LAST ACRE

Let's not spend too much time on this
but if made to choose, would you
say the world bends to human ideas
about beauty? Or that we,
in fact, are made beautiful by
the world, its winds a shade of pink
we haven't learned to see? I think about
smoke, how it finds a way inside
cheeses, honey, and trout. We pay extra
to consume meals so permeated. Now
I want to eat the sky, the trees, blisters
of darkness at a backyard party going late.
Usually I turn toward magic, but today
it's yeast. Fermentation as proof
transformation is possible. This leads
naturally to the last acre of emptiness
where the subdivision gives way
to what it was once: an open field
simmering in the nacreous breath
of a summer moon. This must be where
we return on our knees to the altar
that banged us into being. One pan
forged of lightning, one washed cold
in a river. What a noise it must have made
long ago. It's not just me saying this.
It's our wildness, and it wants so much
to teach us who we are.

LANDING AT NIGHT

Our descent, wiped through the cloud deck.
Straight-backed school children, eyes forward.

We are well behaved. We are good.
We say it is fine

to be human, to depend on steel
for buoyancy. Our spines

radio signals below, to the lives
we have lived, sloughed

from each of our bodies like ghosts
left behind. In this city,

an orchard of starlight below,
a thousand glassine

you's and *me's* wait in all the rooms
we've ever been in. As we, aloft,

watch the seatbelt signs
line up in single file constellations

pointing the way home, back into
the warm sheaf of selves

that will sleep, tonight, a body
once in attendance again.

THE LIGHT IN FLORENCE

I've been sitting at Piazzale Michelangelo
overlooking this clay tile kingdom
every afternoon for 25 years.

I've seen how the sun sails in
from eastern Oz
by way of
Never-Neverland.

I've learned how often beauty and place
choose each other, and leave us
to furnish the moment.
Lucky the café chairs know

to line up, elbow to elbow, in time
for the matinee: An adventure of light
chasing the Arno right into the heart

of the city. Up the wide slope of hill
to this encampment in the body
of a junior year abroad.

As the minutes mount a campaign
and the horizon sorts color
by genus and phylum,

we can write letters
to the afternoon and to the river.

We can draw a map
to brightness, taste the burn
of espresso.

We can see when the naked
armies of David figurines retreat
dutifully with their vendors.

Whether they too
go in the direction of silence.

POWERS

To evade red dodge balls aimed
his way, he learns to be faint.
To empty himself, of his self.

Like the Invisible Woman
who wills herself to vanish,
becomes an ivory shadow

amid comic-book crimson
and turquoise, her dotted line
here, and not here, simultaneously,

he lays his small body on concrete
to trace his form in chalk. First
the feet, then the legs. Up one side

and down the other. Outlines
each contour, and copies himself
in friction and dust, a version

transparent enough to slip

from panel to panel.

LIFEGUARD

Synchronous whistles
at the three o'clock break.
I hoist myself poolside
and drip. Cross arms to hide
thin ribs stacked like saltines.

He descends from his tower
to the concrete. Muscles pull
the upstroke of his spine
as he stretches. Arms curve
parentheses around the sky.

Then he swings each one in hoops
until they're loose in their sockets.
Breath swells under clavicle serifs.
Red trunks hip-hung
on a swath of skin, pale

below his sepia abdomen.
Mirrored shades volley light and smiles
from girls standing by.
When his lips part
his teeth dare the sun.

Cold and shrunken inside my suit
I pull threads from my towel. Worry
want might sprout like hair under arms.
Barely fourteen, too timid
to try-out for JV,

I watch him dive into blue.
Body bending a comma
beneath the surface. His fingers
skim the secret slick
of the drain's open mouth.

VIEW OF THE FAIRWAY

They'd been walking; it was something to do

at sixteen when evening skimmed
across the Minnesota prairie
to their little college town. A cottony wind

swept the humid hours away
with the late-waning sun.
She called after dinner. He left home

and turned toward hers, walked past
flickering television-lit windows, laugh tracks
blending with cricket calls, until he saw her

under an ochre cone of lamp light
on a sidewalk halfway in between.
They talked low and wandered

along the edge of the golf course,
took each other's hand and ventured
step by step into darkness.

Across temporarily abandoned lawns,
up to a little rise on the 16th tee
where they sat and watched

shadowy shapes of trees on sable grasses
overlap in a collage of construction paper scenery,
scissor-fringed pine branches

waving in the pitch, star-flecked
glitter on the page and moon-glow
pooling like glue in the sand traps.

They fell asleep there, together
on the grass. They did not dream
of the future, of the damage and joy

that would be drawn and torn
in the space of another decade or two.
They woke to daylight

and a whole world
cut from fresh sheets
of yellow, blue and green.

LATE SUMMER

Tonight's moon has dropped its shawl.
    I'm in the yard again, waiting

for the air to crawl out from under the ferns
    where it has been hiding

all day, cheek to mud.
    This communion with stillness,

a simple arrangement
    for the willing—

Want nothing, and the dark
    will lessen the distance

between your body and its own
    as a rabbit sometimes will

when hungry or untroubled enough
    to come very close—

herald from some quieter place
    breathing beside us.

ARRIVAL

Some mornings, the only choice is to yield

to the guide in Munich who knows the way to go on
begins underground, with an introduction by subway

to a city I'd never call home. Passing through stations
just long enough to read the names and wonder

what's waiting past each yawn of double doors?
I wasn't listening. But signaled, I followed the others

off the train, through the tunnel and its echoes,
onto an escalator that rose from the station

and parted the cobbles at Marienplatz,
where the sun was shining on other students

and tourists waiting for the Glockenspiel.
There's a movie where all escalators ascend

forever skyward to something like heaven,
and when I felt my chin tip up, as if by the hand

of some benevolent ghost, I saw flowers
spilling red over red, over windows and centuries

of soot on the gothic towers of the Rathaus.
Sometimes, a summer sky

pushes every beautiful possible forward,
right into the body, and through.

AMERIKANER ABROAD

At twenty he might have been newborn,
        a vampire who'd flown all night

to this once imagined place
        finally seen and touched. Here,

his voice nearly drained
        of words, of blood, he was hungry

to survive inside strangeness.
        What better invitation

to be reborn, remade
        for a year at least? Be a body

undone from breath by one
        fluent in the same form of

to want. A kiss was waiting
        inside an afternoon, three months

away, waiting in the mouth
        of a boy waiting in a room,

waiting for him to say
        yes.

MEMORY & THE BODY

Warmed gradually by the sun,
memory merges with the body

that folds the towels, tastes butter
melting into bread, seals lines of sympathy
in a card. Like two trees

in the way trees sometimes grow into
one another. A phenomenon called
*inosculation. To join as one. To unite
intimately.*

Body bends memory to fit
inside a closing crevice,
allowing only some
keeping.

Memory runs through the body
like sap, a kind of belief
that makes this living feel

somehow real, somehow inevitable
as spring.

When trees inosculate, they become
a *gemel*, a pair entwined by shared fiber.
Indistinguishable. A guidance
to the same self within.

TOO EARLY TO TELL ALL SECRETS

Sometimes in a nest
of shredded newspaper.

Sometimes polished in pink
or canary-colored shells.

Sometimes in a shallow bowl
where they roll around

like marbles or gum balls,
or eggs, right up to the rim

and back in. Up
to the lip, tempting

to skip the limit and crack
open on the table,

available and sticky.

THIS MIGHT SUSTAIN US

I thought it was brave,
inviting you to breakfast.

Our shoulders tent above the table
as our knees skirmish below.
You brought the paper; I brought my appetite.
This is what people do, I think

as coffee arrives. I pass the cream
and wait for the spoon. There is only one
spoon. The waitress brings your plate

piled with potatoes and promises
mine will be just a minute. *Go ahead*

I insist, *Begin while it's hot*.
When the smell of the steam
makes you smile. *Go on, go ahead*.
Sample the patty as it sweats

on the ceramic. Split the yolk,
watch it gush and glisten and cling

to the tines of the fork. Sop it up
with a corner of crust and lick
jelly right from your thumb. *Damn*

what a mouth. Damn
what a meal.

TOURISTS AT DUOMO DI SIENA

At first, and for a long time, the tongue lies
flat inside the vestibule of the mouth,
as if stripped of the luxury of language.

Centuries of cool air quieting inside
the stone walls and columns remind us
that scale, like belief, must be felt in the body

to be understood. High sails of marble
embark in all directions across the ceiling,
made more of a miracle by knowing

such grace was engineered by the hands
of humans, whose bodies, like stars,
died before the light completed its curve.

Yet we fail to hold grandeur close enough
after a while. We must be told to notice:
The sculpted faces along the perimeter

repeat. The pink seams in the floor mosaics
lying shattered before our shoes. The combustion
of gold and light in the cathedral dome.

Eventually, many of us wonder, how long before it's okay
to confess hunger or simple exhaustion
with the responsibility of awe?

Released to the rain-washed cobbles
on the piazza, we are sold postcards
to write our life's story.

CLOSER TO THE MOUNTAIN

When it comes to touching strangers, even
casual acquaintances—to finesse attention or
to emphasize a point—the only permissible way
is lightly at the elbow. According to experts
all else is too familiar, because above, the bicep
curls inward like a mollusk, and too far down
risks skin, a waiting palm. So when I reached for you
in the crowded atrium today, the gesture small
enough to go unnoticed, I was surprised. I suppose
it had been a while for me, or maybe it was
the strange warmth of your youth, imported
from another continent (the accent and the silk
darkness or your beard). I kept it light as snow
gathering on a shrub. Soft as the inner fold
of a towel, or the unturned pages of a left-open
book. Here is my body on earth, in a room,
next to you. For a moment at rest, and
without words. A species closer to the mountain
goats or wild ponies. Pair of bison standing
in a cloud of our shared breath, hearts
slowing when we draw close.

BORROWED

The bar is full of beautiful children
drinking pints of beer. The young and pretty

men wear chinos. Rolled up
shirtsleeves expose soft pine

forearms. Beards are in fashion
this year, and clean haircuts combed

to the nape with sandalwood pomade.
They talk of hops and brewer's yeast

as if they know something about
the lives they're supposed to be living.

They love or do not love the young women
seated at pub tables that have been here since

before they were born. The girls tolerate talk
of expensive bikes and recent *films*. The boys'

impossible eyelashes. The girls adjust
thick scarves into cowls around the pale

tracery of their necks. Hairclips
and plastic eyeglass frames

in turquoise, tangerine, rose.
It's that kind of college place.

It's that kind of night: everyone trades
one life for another with glances

around the room. Everyone wants
to order another round.

YOU MUST BE TOLD YOU ARE A FIREFIGHTER

People neglect to mention this addendum
when discussing the career plans of children.
But you can't go wandering the neighborhood
at any hour of day or night just hoping
to see sparks fly from the shingles of a rambler.
Like some convenient need you came
ready to meet with a garden hose and hatchet.

More often someone comes along, comes
right up to you and says, *Okay, now. Now
you are a real ---*. It happens all the time:
*You're a very good cook. Congratulations
you're a licensed barber. You're a first-grader
today. You're quite a smooth talker.*

Wouldn't it be something
if more often we made it a point
to call each other some terrific thing
we didn't know we already are?

You're the Wizard of Weeknight Dinners
the way you make a meal of whatever's in the pantry.

You're my Holly Golightly. You understand
"the Mean Reds" and like a good pastry.

He's as lucky as *Coins in the Fountain Gone Green*.
She's the *Docent of Pho* in this city.
You've always been *Apricots in the Backyard of Childhood*.

Imagine the Halloween costumes, the business cards
we'd get to carry. Finally knowing.

NEW TERRITORY

Instead of rabbits in the yard,
an old tiger in the driveway
sprawled on the concrete

as an April moon washes its face
in puddles up and down the alley.
From the dark, a roar, a howl

of an airplane overhead, of a dog
behind a neighbor's fence. Neither disturbs
this supine weight, this late hunger

I name my restless want,
the practiced muscle of it
worked to ropey strength.

Between the black, a truth
shines in brass: I've lived
long enough, killed enough

of myself, waiting to believe
in the power to be some other
thing. To decide

what is real. In light, language,
old gods starving in the dark.
Tonight, I assume this sinew

as survival, its fierce magic.
Part birth, part becoming
a curious shiver of new.

DEER, AS IN A DREAM

Past a village of tiled kiosks
selling oranges, hard rolls, espresso
in tiny paper cups, sleepy travelers

shuffle down the platform, to the closer edge
of midnight, where trains sheened in new frost
wait to take them in, and take them on.

When beyond the farthest rail, a deer
steps through the whitened ditch grass
as if lifted into view

by the pale arc beneath its belly.
Jet eyes and nose tuning toward
lit windows on the train

where passengers busy with baggage
find their places for the night. *Look there!*
pleads a night voice. Not the PA

system static or exhausted vendors
working hour twelve. Maybe the station
itself. *A deer! As if it walked out of a—*

but all eyes remain fixed
on oranges cradled in hands. Still
someone here knows

that this—this
is wonderful. *Look now.* This is all
about to change.

THREE

GOING SOMEWHERE

Then one night, side by side
in bed, we closed our eyes
and breathed inside our room.
At four a.m. we rose. Stars
fastened but fading. We opened
a door to cold, and dragged
suitcases down the walk.
The plastic wheels caught
in the newly fallen snow.

GIVEN HONEY IN THE DARK

The deck out back kneels low in the grass.
Wood planks worn soft with rain and sun,
ten thousand human footprints.
Picture someone's old Christmas lights
unboxed and strung up—in June!—from the gutters
to the lowest birch branch, and reaching up
to tether an ark of stars.

I meet the hostess standing barefoot in the grass.
She takes a chilled bottle of white from my hand
and replaces it with the warm palm of her brother
the graduate student, in town to write his dissertation.
Well, trying to write, he says. *So far summer's been
swimming with my nephews and niece, watching t-ball games.*
And standing under trees at parties, his collar open
at the throat to catch the gold and green
dripping from the bulbs above.

He leads me to two open seats
at a table under the tree.
We pass cold tomato salad, plates
of marinated meat, and peaches
tiger-striped from the grill.

I ask about his field. *Fractal geometry,*
he says, *Certain equations can replicate patterns
found in nature.* In the fronds of ferns, for example.
Tree growth over time. A whole forest.
Maybe equation draws the pattern. Or maybe pattern
wrote the equation. *One way or the other, it can tell us
the shape of what's next.*
                           And he's right. Everywhere
artichoke leaves overlap. The weave of the tablecloth repeats.

The evening pleats in on itself. Gathers its dark heat
closer to our end of the table and this slow dessert:
small bowls of vanilla ice cream, with almonds glazed in honey.
When a sliver of almond sticks to my lip, the grad student
brushes it away with his thumb. Leaving my mouth to wonder
if it has been kissed or stung.

MOON STORIES

One appeared a young pirate
on the bow of the galaxy.

One shoveled stars to the burning
mouths of tigers in the engine room.

That long summer of lime and gin
on the deck past sunset,

we watched oil-drip batwings
rag overhead, and beyond

the soft-woven skies of late June
beginning to thicken, we witnessed:

A rounded belly settle in robes of fog
to wait for its supper of prayers.

A Cheshire grin swing low enough
we reached for the trapeze.

Come August and another bottle
emptied, when a pale slit

eyed us drunken mice, we couldn't remember
which of us had started the game,

so we raised our glasses—cool and wet
in our palms—and shook

softening crescents of ice
onto the thirsty lawn.

DRIVING IN WEST ST. PAUL, WHICH IS SOUTH OF ST. PAUL BUT WEST OF SOUTH ST. PAUL

What part of the city is this?
I asked, suspicious that the GPS
was playing cat's cradle with us.

It's a mystery, you said, looking past
the windshield to a handful of pennies
tossed on the road, a disruption of light

along that bluff above where the river
flexes against its banks, and voluminous
greens arch backs to indigo hands

reaching out from the dusk. Not so
very long ago, you and I were both
infants. Crazy, isn't it? Those bodies

became these bodies. The wet little yolks
of our souls lived unsettled inside
a nest of new ribs. We slept

unaware the runny things
would have to sustain us
for a lifetime. Maybe longer.

What did we think? Waking
inside this simmer of bright
to a world—unnamed, wild,

endless with bruise and flowers,
blizzard, chrome, darkness
thick as syrup. Heat dance

behind the curtain, sour light
and so much beyond reach.
Of course we cried. And then

we continued on. Seeing
what we would see. Going
where we could go.

THE NIGHT WATCHMAN ENDS HIS SHIFT

Plucks down the round moon, socks it away
in a clean cotton drawstring sack that he hangs
from a peg high on the wall.

Harvests bushels of stars
in baskets and buckets; sets them
shining in the hall, where yesterday's
storm-rinsed sunset
drains in a tub.

Calls the owls
home to their cupboards
and checks that the bats
have folded and tucked
themselves, wing to wing,
into their suede-lined drawers.

Time to snuff street lamps and hush
the tired moths. Time to collapse
the dark canopy of sky
like a tent.

Gather-up wisps of sleep
in armfuls of party streamers
pulled from tree branches.
A dozen blackbirds
scream across the sky, paste dark
flecks that fall away

in the brushing light. Still
the pouched moon glows
faintly against the sky-blue wall,
too thrilled to sleep. Everywhere

doors open and open and open.

COOKING PASTA FOR MY PARENTS

Tonight I gather the constellations
of chopped onions on the cutting board
into a glistening mound between my palms.

On the stove: two pans bright as mirrors
collect the stray thoughts that come
from inching food closer to the table.
In the next room

someone is watching *60 Minutes*.
Someone is making a list

of what to pack, what to sell, beneficiaries to name.
How small those letters, how neat

those lines. *What is life anyway if not
unwanted thoughts at inopportune moments?*
These words had been lodged in my mind

going on three days, and I decided to decide
it was truest thing I'd ever heard, even if
I was the one who said it. At least I think I

said it, or thought it, or wrote it in the margin

next to a graph of life expectancies by generation.
Useless information. Show me the chances: if it'll

come quick, a slip, a scalpel's nick. Or in weeks passed
one half-lipped spoonful at a time. Raise the flames

and wait. Stare down a new refrigerator and my fifth
decade bright with birds trailing crayon spirals
drawn by nieces. They're an age when time feels long

or so I remember. Now mine's half over and yet
midlife is a myth, I remind myself.

No one actually knows the midpoint
until after, when the math no longer matters.
My mid could have been years ago, and I'll die tomorrow
or the next moment as I stand here watching

pale mushroom slices fall away from the blade
like phases of the moon. There's nothing left to do
but crush the garlic, check the water on the stove.

Has it boiled? Is it close? The onions are
as the recipe instructs—soft and turning
golden as miniature gems.

NOT WHEN THE MILK

At the office, when a framed poster declares
"if you're not moving forward, you're dying in place"
I begin to argue while the coffee brews.

By now, the contours of time have delivered me
to the center of a life, where I have found
the beginning of all things. I still march

a straight line through weekdays like everyone,
but the cliff we're headed toward worries me
more than any place I might linger. And so

I think about levitation a lot, assume a yogi pose
with crossed legs, back straight, to feel how much
the world radiates outward from me

when I'm in this mood. It's a very modern office
with a dedicated space inside for bicycles
and tall unobstructed windows to baptize

all the young people calling themselves entrepreneurs.
My beef with the poster is no doubt related
to another bad habit: critiquing the anonymous

authors of signage, ad copy, chalkboards in restaurants.
It makes me a bore to everyone discussing the apps
disrupting an industry. (You're supposed to agree that's interesting.)

Also, it wastes my time, this policing of grammar
and bickering with posters. All words are imperfect.
Every expression we conjure has flaws

so is there any use in arguing? Not when the milk
pours its cold white into your mug, its impossible
love every morning you're dying in place.

A RARE FIND

Some summers they turn up
like agates under the hammock.

It's that kind of luck, to find a day
without clocks, only sunlight.

When no one is waiting for you to show up
and say witty, intelligent things.

The trees above you do not know the word
Tuesday. So it begins to step away, slowly,

through that gathering of saplings,
beyond the inhabited world.

Now you will swing, you will doze,
you will dream

you are a pony on the sunny side
of the pen. So many hours

left in the day, and already
every necessary thing accomplished.

MAPS

Nobody ever finds a way out of the forest
of time. Like Hansel and Gretel at an impasse

my sister and I tell very different stories
about childhood. Cool shadows follow

that path we shared but no longer
see the same.

BECAUSE THEY ARE MINE, I WISH TO VISIT

As if they were goats at a hobby farm
ready to press their sun-warmed
foreheads to my hand.

As if they were shells, feathers, found stones
collected under the hinged lid of a box.
Waiting to be examined, known. Oh—

I've been to the movies
I've seen all the trouble

time travel incites: how it strains
continuity, the fraying of logic
undone from the linear. Still

one look was not enough.

I want to go back, to see again
all my days that have been.

Build me a clock with hands that spin
time in roulette, each stop a surprise

to work, to third grade, to prom. First sight

of ocean after hours in the car. Kissing
in the basement. London 1993. That ski trip
in junior high when somehow, everyone
got along. The luck of it:

Summer vacation, Flintstones cartoons,
Rice Krispies in milk. Then hours behind

branches and shade, where the lilacs grew tall
and thick by the fence. To crawl across dirt
damp under palms, a little space

hidden in a hidden day.

I know the risk, the wounds
waiting to come. If it's the day
of the accident, the fight

that ends the friendship, the very last
visit to the vet. Is it masochistic
to think

I can handle such loss
as if from a distance? Still,

I keep a large wardrobe
in varying sizes: wedding suit,
onesie, T-ball uniform. In case

one day fantasy becomes
technology, making real
the chance to return

to this particular scatter of light
broken across the polished wood floor.

POSTSCRIPT

After years spent staring out
windows of coffee shops
alone and walking lost
in the park in refusal
of answering the phone,

I'm sprinting home

like a neighbor child
through the dark yards
to flicker-switch
the porch lamp and signal
safe arrival, in a place

where my morning smile
spreads like a puddle
and I stand as a radio tower
broadcasting invisibly, invisibly—
I'm new, I'm a party guest

learning to salsa dance
in an unfinished basement
beneath the gathering
snow, turning and turning
while the orange marble of my life
glows warm on my tongue
and I do my best

to avoid collision
with the idle washer/dryer.

NOVEMBER, MINNEAPOLIS

And then, a morning like this: new snow
with just enough stick—every tree
limb and finger, follicle and lash
coated in white. Every needle of pine

and each swaying cord of that lone
willow dreaming of a riverbank. Sky
just beginning to blue, and for an hour
it's like walking into forgiveness.

It's true about the impossibility we face,
always trying so hard to prepare ourselves
for the too-muchness of life. I've tried
for years and still haven't learned

how to really believe
I won't always know
this living crown of cold,
these hands beginning to work.

A COMPLETION

This Goldbergian machine may go on
making toast, air in the bellows,

surge of blood to warm the cheek.
But not forever.

Tens of thousands of cells
shed every hour, somehow,

an invisible loss. Oh,
genesis of understanding, advise me.

Announce in me a completion.
Call it a sown field or a painting

of that sowing. Call the imperfection
love and use it as soldering

to fasten me forever in the grasp
of those I came from, and those

I came to. The wish to be burgundy
and ochre and indigo as well as young

snow beyond the streetlamps
never goes away, does it?

I'm saying it doesn't. I'm saying
my tongue has tasted both iron and snow.

ETYMOLOGY AT DUSK

Tell me I'm not the only one who stands
under the tarnished brass tack
that holds plum-skinned skies aloft.

Tell me you too have listened to a shadow
open like a door to some
unnamed season, felt the air

rush in, smelling of rain. Maybe call it
the soul. Maybe
a wound

that comes from living
enough days
turning toward love, enough nights

toward the face of the moon.
But believe me when I say,
some language must

have a word for, that there was once
an idiom to mean, that someday
soon our tongues will curl perfectly

to fit that feeling when
a million minnows of darkness
school together in the breeze

and pull and pull at that soft
knot of want, always alive
inside the chest.

ART CLASS

Before the world broke apart
into pixels that had to be counted
by the millions, I had one lesson

in a darkroom, that place where
our lights became darks, darks
becoming absences
as each contour burned
lines against a plane. A plain. A field

capable of holding galaxies
star-flecked with promises
of some unknowable peace.
It was tempting,

to hold up the night sky
as some kind of evidence. Proof

that the next
being-alone-in-the-vastness
could begin by closing
newly frosted lashes
for a cold drift through the cosmos.

After the dumb luck to have tripped
on the threshold of this planet,

who's to say? All the oils we are
might float, suspended like inks
in a rinse jar, eager
for a universe

flat as paper, clean as invitation.

Acknowledgments

Thank you to the many teachers and fellow writers who have offered guidance, insights, camaraderie, and encouragement over the years, including: Annie Dawid, Melanie Figg, Christine Sikorski, William Reichard, all the Mac Writers (Aime, Cris, Jill, Jon, Kasey, Patrice, Todd), Kristin Naca, E. Ethelbert Miller, Patricia Weaver Francisco, Jerod Santek, my Loft Mentor Series cohort, Jude Nutter, Deborah Keenan and the Monday Morning Poets, Carolyn Williams-Noren, Michael Kleber-Diggs, Timothy Otte, Jim Moore, my LPP pals (Kathleen, Jan, Kelly), and Gretchen Marquette.

Special thanks to Merie Kirby for opening the door to poetry. To Marisha Chamberlain for her enthusiasm. To Andrea and Chandra for that pen in ninth grade. To Thadra and Sue for the nickname. To Margaret Hasse for first suggesting the book's title. And to Jonis Agee and Brent A. Spencer at Brighthorse Books for making this book a reality.

My thanks and love to my family for supporting even my most esoteric of endeavors, as well as to the many wonderful people I'm lucky to call my friends. And always to Bryan, who makes all my days better by far; I love you.

I am also truly grateful to the editors and readers of the following journals and magazines where poems in this collection first appeared (sometimes in different forms):

Poet Lore: "Going Somewhere"

Water~Stone Review: "Given Honey in the Dark," "The Night Watchman Ends His Shift," "Indiana Corn," "Late Radius," "Likelihoods, Sequels and Spinoffs"

Narrative Magazine: "Guest of the Lacuna," "Cooking Pasta for My Parents," "Late Summer," "Last Acre"

FLURRY: "Reservations"

Salamander: "Lifeguard"

Midwestern Gothic: "View of the Fairway," "Borrowed"

The Nassau Review: "Landing at Night"

SHARKPACK Poetry Annual: "Here and Hiding"

Tinderbox Poetry Journal: "A Mischief Within," "X-ray"

Nimrod Poetry Journal: "Powers," "Lodging"

Tampa Review: "Disembark"

Cider Press Review: "In the Garden"

Cimarron Review: "As Language," "Not When the Milk"

LEE COLIN THOMAS lives and writes in Minneapolis, where he is a communications consultant and instructor at the University of Minnesota. Lee's poems have appeared in *Poet Lore, Narrative Magazine, Water~Stone Review, The Gay and Lesbian Review Worldwide, Midwestern Gothic*, and other publications. Online at www.leecolinthomas.net. *Honey in the Dark* is the 2020 winner of the Brighthorse Prize in Poetry.

www.ingramcontent.com/pod-product-compliance
Lightning Source LLC
Chambersburg PA
CBHW030349100526
44592CB00010B/890